W9-CNP-189

THE KNOWLEDGE LIBRARY

FIGHTING MEN
and their
UNIFORMS

THE KNOWLEDGE LIBRARY

FIGHTING MEN and their UNIFORMS

By Kenneth Allen

Illustrated by John Berry

GROSSET & DUNLAP

Publishers · NEW YORK
A National General Company

Published in the United States of America by
Grosset & Dunlap, Inc. New York, N.Y.

FIRST PRINTING 1971
Copyright © 1970, 1971 by The Hamlyn Publishing Group, Ltd.
All Rights Reserved.
Adapted from the Grosset All-Color Guide:
MILITARY UNIFORMS, 1686–1918
Library of Congress Catalog Card Number: 75–156132
ISBN: 0–448–00368–6 (Trade Edition)
ISBN: 0–448–07262–9 (Library Edition)
Printed by Officine Grafiche Arnoldo Mondadori, Verona, Italy.

contents

Page

THE EARLY DAYS OF MILITARY UNIFORMS

Soldiers began to wear distinctive clothing in order to tell immediately who were their friends and who their enemies. The armies of the ancient world – Egyptians, Greeks, Assyrians and Romans – all wore such uniforms. The Romans, particularly, made sure that their military men wore armor and clothing of a "uniform" style. At the same time the Eagle of the Legion was paraded and honored like the battle standards of later times.

During the Middle Ages, knights and their followers wore badges and colors so that they, too, could instantly tell friend from foe. The end of this period marked the rise of mercenaries – men who fought for other countries for pay – especially the Swiss. These men always dressed in similar clothing.

THE FIRST UNIFORMED ARMY

What may be called the first "modern" uniforms began in Sweden. About 1620, Gustavus Adolphus II formed an army which was drilled, equipped and organized on modern lines. His pikemen presented a living steel-tipped hedge to the oncoming enemy; his musketeers, firing by numbers, kept up a continual discharge; his squadrons of cuirassiers charged at the gallop, firing their pistols when within range.

His regiments were called the "Blue," "Yellow" and "Green" from the main color of their clothing.

FRANCE AND HER SOLDIERS

During the reign of Louis XIV, the French cavalry regiments were uniformed in light gray with red facings. Louvois, the King's military adviser, then put the infantry into uniforms as well, so that a fully uniformed army, in the modern sense, came into being. The French regiments wore light gray, the Swiss red, the Germans black, and the Italians blue.

With the introduction of standing armies, uniforms became established, and governed by their own rules and regulations.

Above: Swedish Grenadier, 1700. He wears the tall head-piece known as the miter-cap.

Left: Private, Royal Regiment of Fusiliers. These first escorted the Train of Artillery but later became part of the line as the 7th Foot.
Far left: A matross of the British Train of Artillery. His duty was to fight off attacks by enemy cavalry when the guns were on the move. He holds a linstock, a staff which held a lighted match for firing cannon. In the early days, the guns were not served by regular soldiers but by a train recruited for the campaign.

Below: Russian Dragoon of 1700. He is wearing the three-cornered or tricorne hat. It was first formed by looping up the front of a felt-brimmed hat so that it did not get in the way during arms drill.

THE BEGINNING OF BRITAIN'S ARMY

When Civil War broke out in England in 1642 there was nothing worth calling an army in existence. It seemed as if the king had every advantage. His cavaliers were well trained and skilled horsemen.

The parliamentary forces, on the other hand, were mainly recruited from poorer families. Many had little skill with arms.

THE FIRST BRITISH UNIFORMS

Oliver Cromwell was to change all that. He set about equipping and drilling a regiment of horse. In time it became known as Cromwell's "Ironsides."

Cromwell had seen the cavaliers gallop into action in velvet clothes of all colors and with flowing locks. He was determined that should not happen in *his* army. His men had their hair cut in a short style and were known as Roundheads. Every man also had to wear a scarlet tunic. This stayed as the standard color in the British Army for nearly three centuries.

MARLBOROUGH'S MEN

The scarlet coat from Cromwell's time, together with the tricorne hat, were worn by both Horse and Foot in the army that went with Marlborough to the War of the Spanish Succession.

MARLBOROUGH GOES TO WAR

On May 24, 1650, a son was born to Sir Winston Churchill, a landowner in Dorset. The boy went to St Paul's School in London and then, at fifteen, became page to the Duke of York, heir to the throne. Two years later, young John Churchill joined the Army and became an officer in the Foot Guards. That was the beginning of an army career that was to make him the greatest general of his age.

When Queen Anne came to the throne, she made Churchill – who had become the Duke of Marlborough – Commander-in-Chief. His men soon saw that he cared for their welfare and called him "Corporal John."

BEFORE BLENHEIM

Marlborough was chosen to lead an Anglo-Dutch army against the French in what was to be called the War of the Spanish Succession. The Austrians, commanded by Prince Eugene of Savoy, were Marlborough's allies and together they formed the Grand Alliance. By a series of marches, Marlborough joined forces with Prince Eugene and the combined army made ready to attack the French, under their

Above: Private in a British line regiment, 1704. He is armed with a flintlock musket which had a maximum range of about 229 m and fired two one-ounce balls every minute. The infantry usually held their fire until the enemy was within about 90 m or less.

Socket bayonets came into use about this time. The soldier **above** is shown wearing a bayonet scabbard on his left side. In addition to weapons, Marlborough's "foot-sloggers" also carried a cloak, haversack and cooking-pot.

Left: Unlike the British, the French Army wore standardized uniforms. They were usually white or silver-gray. Holding the musket is a Private of the Regiment de Champagne. The other is a Private of the Regiment Royal. Only cuffs, waistcoats and buttons varied.

proud general, Tallard. The French Army was in a strong position in and around a village on the Danube called Blenheim.

MARLBOROUGH'S GREAT VICTORIES

During the morning of August 13, 1704, the Allied Army moved into position. Marlborough was sharing a hasty meal with his staff when an officer galloped up with the news that the Prince of Savoy was ready to begin the attack. His comment was, "Now gentlemen, to your posts!"

Five minutes later the roar of battle sounded from one end of the plain of Hochstadt to the other.

The attack was begun by the British infantry. They were met by a murderous cross-fire which forced them to draw back. French cavalry came thundering down on them but they were saved by the arrival of Wyndham's Horse (later the 6th Dragoon Guards) and by the second line of infantry.

By nightfall, the French surrendered, having lost 20,000 men. General Camille Tallard was taken prisoner. When he congratulated Marlborough on beating the finest troops in the world, he received the dry reply; "I think mine must be the best . . . they have beaten yours!"

This great British general went on to win three more outstanding victories – Ramillies, Oudenarde and Malplaquet.

Above: Private of the 1st Foot Guards, 1704. Marlborough began his military career in this regiment as an ensign in 1667. Thirty-seven years later he chose it to lead the attack on the Schellenberg at Blenheim. The Foot consisted of four battalions of Guards. These were the 1st and 2nd Foot, the Coldstreams and the Scots. There were also line regiments known by the names of their commanding officers. Indeed, these colonels were the virtual owners of their units. They even sold commissions within them to officers.

Left: Private in the Walloon Regiment, Austrian Infantry, 1707. All the men of the Walloon Foot Guards came from the Netherlands, which was then part of the Austrian Empire.

Walloons come from southern Belgium. The green coat the Private is wearing was unusual among the scarlet and blue of the rest of the Allies. It was, however, general in all the eight Netherlandish regiments which were then in the Austrian service. In 1708, at the time of the Battle of Oudenarde, all infantry regiments based in Austria and Hungary went into "pearl-white" coats.

THE BATTLE OF FONTENOY

In 1745, during the War of Austrian Succession, an Allied Army of British, Austrian and Dutch troops once again faced a French army. The armies prepared for battle near a small village called Fontenoy.

The Allies were commanded by the Duke of Cumberland, the French by General Maurice de Saxe. Louis XV of France and the fifteen-year-old Dauphin came to watch the battle.

THE BATTLE BEGINS ...

The Austrians and Dutch were to attack the French right flank, the British, the center. The English Guards advanced until they were facing the French Guards. Lord May commanding the former shouted to the enemy to open fire. Back came the answer: "We never fire first. The honor is yours!" The English did so, killing many of the French.

... AND ENDS

The Dutch and Austrians were thrown back and, at the vital moment, Saxe put in his reserves, which included the Irish Brigade. The British were suddenly forced to withdraw, taking their colors with them.

Above: One of de Ligne's Dragoons, a Walloon unit within the Austrian Army.

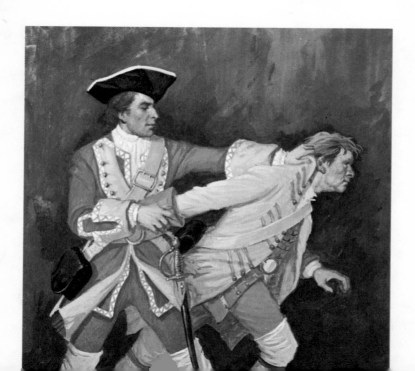

Left: Private of the British 13th Foot brings in a French prisoner for questioning. The Frenchman, wearing the standard silver-gray uniform, is of the crack Regiment of the King.

BRITAIN FIGHTS FOR CANADA

As early as 1497, England and France were exploring parts of North America. By 1606 the colonization of Virginia by England had begun. In 1620 the *Mayflower* arrived with the Pilgrim Fathers. Very soon, England and France quarreled over their boundaries and local skirmishes grew into a full scale war.

EARLY DEFEATS

In 1754, British colonists, aided by Virginians under a young officer named George Washington, were forced to surrender. Regular troops were sent to avenge this defeat. The British were not used to forest warfare, however, and in their red coats and white cross-belts they were easy targets for hidden French and Indian marksmen.

This was the first of many defeats the British were to suffer at the hands of the French in North America.

THE GREAT VICTORY

In 1759 an army of colonists was raised; a strong British force was sent to assist them and Canada was invaded. This led to the capture of Quebec, after which France gave up all claims to territory in Canada.

Above: British Marine in 1756. His cap (*shown above him*) was similar to, but smaller than that of the Grenadiers, which earned him the French nickname of "The Little Grenadier." The marines were originally The Lord Admiral's Maritime Regiment and were raised in 1664.

Right: Private of the 60th Foot. This was raised in New York as the Royal American Regiment and became the 60th in 1757. One of its battalions was dressed in green for skirmishing. This was so successful that the whole regiment changed to the same color which gave it its name — Green Jackets.
Far right: Private of Roger's Rangers, shown wearing the green of the forest.

THE SEVEN YEARS' WAR

Frederick I of Prussia liked "playing soldiers." Only his were real. He took raw recruits, dressed them in magnificent uniforms, then drilled them until they moved almost like automatons. But their bravery and skill as marksmen were unequalled.

BRITAIN JOINS PRUSSIA

The countries around Prussia soon became alarmed at its growing might. They formed a coalition which included France, Austria, Russia, Sweden and smaller states. War broke out in 1757 and Britain sided with the new king of Prussia, Frederick the Great, against France.

A British-Hanoverian army, commanded by the Duke of Cumberland, was defeated at Hastenbeck. The Duke was replaced by Prince Ferdinand of Brunswick, who had already won a great victory at Rossbach. Six regiments of infantry and six of cavalry were sent from England as reinforcements.

The French Army under the Marquis de Contades captured the town of Minden on the Weser. This action threatened the Allies' supply lines and Ferdinand decided to attack the French camp south of Minden, although it was almost impregnable.

Above: Private of the Prussian Regiment von Schwerin, 1757. He wears the traditional tricorne hat of a Prussian musketeer. The light companies within Prussian regiments were known as fusiliers. This came from the word "fusil," or "fusee," a better and more expensive type of musket.

Left: Officer of the British 11th Dragoons, 1756. At Minden, the greatest Allied victory of the Seven Years' War, Lord George Sackville, the commander of the cavalry on the right wing would not give the order to advance. After the battle he was sent back to England in disgrace.

Far left: Officer of the British 24th Foot, 1756. British regiments such as this fought side by side during the Seven Years' War with regiments of the Hanoverian Army. They served under British commanders, for George I, II, III and IV, and also William IV, were rulers of Hanover as well as Britain. The Hanoverian infantry were very similar in appearance to the British, even to the scarlet coats. The main difference was that they wore mustaches while the British were clean-shaven!

Above: Cavalryman of the 8th Prussian Hussars, 1758. Hussars were light cavalry units. The name comes from the Hungarian word *huszar* meaning twentieth man – the one man in twenty picked by ballot for military service. The hussar wore a busby, or high cylindrical cloth cap, a jacket with heavy braiding and a dolman, or pelisse. This was a loose coat worn hanging from the left shoulder.

THE BATTLE OF MINDEN

By a clever maneuver, Prince Ferdinand drew the French Army away from its strong position and into open ground. Contades was furious at being tricked, but had to stand and fight. The battle began at five o'clock in the morning of August 1, 1759. The British infantry, flanked by battalions of Hanoverian and Hessian Foot Guards, advanced boldly to attack the enemy's left wing where the best of the French cavalry was posted.

INFANTRY VERSUS CAVALRY

The Allied battalions pushed forward, marching straight for the French cavalry – an action unheard of in battle. The horsemen drew their sabers and galloped down upon the ranks of plodding infantry. The foot held their fire until the cavalry were almost upon them. Then a rolling volley sent men and horses tumbling in their hundreds. Another charge was made but this, too, was met by a hail of bullets. As if this was not enough, the infantry continued to move forward, bayonets fixed, straight at the shaken Household Cavalry of France. Finally, unable to face the dogged infantry, the cavalry streamed from the field. By ten o'clock, after five hours of fighting, the French Army was in retreat. Had the British Cavalry then advanced, as ordered, the French Army would have been driven right out of Germany!

Right: Infantry Private in the French Regiment of Touraine.
Far right: Private in the Swiss Regiment of Diesbach. A number of such regiments were loaned to France during the Seven Years' War. At Rossbach, in 1757, the battle was really over and the French were defeated, but the Swiss would not yield. Frederick asked, "What are those red brick walls which my artillery cannot breach?" Upon being told they were the Swiss Regiments of Diesbach and Planta, he raised his hat in tribute to their courage.

AMERICA FIGHTS FOR INDEPENDENCE

Above: British Light Infantry helmet of the 5th Foot, about 1775.

To help pay the enormous cost of the Seven Years' War, Britain began to tax her colonies in America. The colonists objected strongly to these taxes and finally showed their anger on the night of December 16, 1773. A group of men from Boston, disguised as Indians ran down to Griffin's Wharf and threw about 340 chests of best Indian tea into the harbor.

This act was punished by Britain who closed the harbor to trade. She also sent a number of red-coated soldiers to the city to see that there were no more incidents.

THE SHOOTING AT LEXINGTON

The American War of Independence really began during the night of April 18, 1775, when a group of British soldiers were seen marching out of Boston. They were on their way to a village called Concord, where they intended to destroy an illegal store of arms. They had to pass through Lexington, the inhabitants of which had to be warned. A young Boston patriot, Paul Revere, galloped through the night on a borrowed horse with the message, "The British are coming!"

Above: Officer, British 17th Light Dragoons, 1775. Dragoons had been in existence in Britain for more than a century. They were originally horsemen armed with a carbine decorated with a dragon's head. From this they got the name Dragoons and formed the medium cavalry of the British Army. The light dragoons were used mainly for scouting and patrol work although they were also useful in action. At Emsdorf, during the Seven Years' War, the 15th Light Dragoons captured sixteen French colors, nine guns and nearly 1,700 prisoners. The 16th and 17th Light Dragoons were chosen for service in America. The 17th wore a badge on their helmet shaped like a skull. It was worn to commemorate the death of General James Wolfe at Quebec in 1759.

At dawn the next morning the redcoats were moving through Lexington, where they saw a colonial militia drilling on the green. Shots were exchanged and some colonists fell. Hostilities had begun!

BOSTON UNDER SIEGE

The redcoats had to fight their way back to Boston. News of the skirmish at Lexington soon spread all over the New England states. Before long, other colonists were arriving to surround Boston where the British were almost in a state of siege.

The colonists had plenty of rifles, but were short of artillery. Then someone remembered that there were guns in the fort at Ticonderoga. Vermont's Green Mountain Boys, led by Ethan Allen, stormed the fort, the garrison surrendered, and guns were soon rumbling toward Boston.

Other local victories were won and then there came the first big challenge. The British, under General Thomas Gage, had abandoned Bunker Hill on the outskirts of the city and the American troops had occupied it. But more British generals arrived in Boston, and they were determined to win it back again.

After an hour-and-a-half of fierce fighting, the hill was recaptured. But out of 3,000 attackers, half were killed or wounded. This was a British victory, but the price was a high one to pay.

Above: Private of the Hessian Regiment Erbprinz, 1776. When the Revolutionary War in America first began, Britain had few regular troops. Reinforcements sent in 1776 included the Hessian Grenadiers, mercenary soldiers from the German state of Hesse-Cassel. There were 22,000 troops altogether, hired to King George III by Frederick II at a cost of more than £3,000,000.

Left: At sunrise on the morning of April 19, 1775, British soldiers on their way to Concord saw American Minutemen (volunteers) on the Common at Lexington. British Major John Pitcairn ordered them to disperse, but an unknown soldier opened fire. Other redcoats also fired, without orders, and eight Americans were killed.

Above: Officer of the British 15th Foot, 1776. This regiment, which was very active in America, became the East Yorkshire Regiment. It had fought in all of Marlborough's four battles. From 1758 until 1815 it was stationed in North America or the West Indies.

INDEPENDENCE

The Continental Congress met and appointed George Washington to lead the first American Army. By March 17, 1776 he had forced the British to evacuate Boston. His next military goal was the city of New York. Even as the British were still boarding their ships in Boston harbor, he sent part of his army marching south and his men occupied the city without any opposition. While they were there, the word "independence" began to be heard for the first time.

On July 4, 1776, Congress adopted the famous Declaration of Independence.

NEW YORK BURNS

While the colonists were celebrating this exciting new sense of freedom, British men-of-war were gliding into New York Bay. It was not long before fresh troops from Britain were landing on Staten and Long Islands. Redcoats and colonists fought and Washington was forced to fall back with his disheartened troops. Fighting continued in and around New York. On September 12, 1776 much of the city was destroyed by fire.

A number of battles followed. These included an attack on Fort Washington on Manhatten Island. Here a charge was made by a Hessian regiment with two Highland regiments, the 43rd and 71st. They were supported by the main British Army under Lord William Howe. The defenders fought gallantly, but were forced to retreat at last.

"GENTLEMAN JOHNNY" ARRIVES

The winter of 1776 passed and spring brought another British general with reinforcements from Canada. He was General John Burgoyne, known in the ranks as "Gentleman Johnny". On July 6, 1777 he recaptured Ticonderoga and forced the colonists to retreat. He followed them keeping his dwindling army trudging towards Albany.

He hoped to make contact with a force moving toward him from New York. But they were not to meet. An American army of 11,000 men under Horatio Gates met Burgoyne's army of less than 5,000.

More than 400 British officers and men were left either dead or wounded. Burgoyne was forced to surrender. It was a significant American victory.

THE FIGHTING CONTINUES

Prior to his victory at Fort Washington, Howe had defeated Washington at the Battle of Brandywine, on September 11, 1777. He then went on to take Philadelphia, which was later recaptured by the colonists, aided by the French, with whom they had formed an alliance. The British were forced to retreat to New York. In June, 1778, a battle was fought at Monmouth, New Jersey, neither side gaining the advantage.

This was followed by the capture of Stony Point, a British stronghold which the colonists captured with fixed bayonets and unloaded muskets.

THE SURRENDER AT YORKTOWN

In January, 1781, the Americans won the Battle of the Cowpens, S.C. This was followed by a British victory at Guilford Courthouse, N.C. After this action, however, the British general, Charles Cornwallis retired to Yorktown, where he was blockaded by a French fleet and besieged by the American and French armies.

The small town was strongly fortified but the combined forces slowly began to push the British back from the outer defenses. The ground they captured enabled them to take up positions from which they could command the whole town. Shells and bombs poured into Yorktown. Cornwallis was forced to surrender. Peace talks began, and in 1783 a treaty was signed which recognized that the thirteen states were no longer under British rule.

Below left: Private in Vermont's volunteer American regiment, the Green Mountain Boys, 1776. At first they were little more than a handful of backwoodsmen, but in May, 1775, under Ethan Allen, they captured Fort Ticonderoga, near Lake Champlain.
Below center: Private, 1st New York Regiment, 1775. Known as McDougall's, its dark blue coat with red facings was typical of most American infantry units.
Below right: Officer, Rhode Island Artillery. Unlike most, which wore blue coats similar to the British, men of this corps sported brown coats with red facings.

IN THE DAYS OF NAPOLEON

At its peak, the army commanded by Napoleon Bonaparte was the largest, the best drilled and the finest uniformed in Europe. Yet it had not always been so. When he was a twenty-seven-year-old general commanding troops of the French Revolution, he took over the French Army in Italy. He found that his men had "neither shoes nor coats nor shirts, and empty magazines."

Yet such was his brilliance that with men like this he routed the Austrians and entered Milan in triumph. With such men he marched more than seventy miles and fought three battles in four days.

In 1797 he invaded Austria and made that country sign a treaty that gave France a great deal of territory. His men were devoted to him and, with new heart, swore they would follow him anywhere.

He then took an army to Egypt where he wanted

Above: Private of the British 4th Foot or the King's Own Regiment. This regiment served with great distinction during the Spanish war against France, when they helped to chase Joseph Bonaparte out of Spain. He wears a cylindrical shako — or stove-pipe cap.

Right: Private, 92nd Highlanders. In 1798 this regiment became more familiarly known as the Gordon Highlanders. They fought splendidly at the battle of Quatre Bras, where at one time they were led by the Duke of Wellington himself. They suffered heavy losses in this battle and their colonel, Cameron of Fassifern was killed.

Far right: Color-sergeant, 9th Foot, 1814. This regiment also served with gallantry in the Peninsular Wars. They became known as the "Holy Boys" because the Spaniards thought their crest of Britannia was that of the Virgin Mary.

to build a new French Empire. But he was cut off from home when Horatio Nelson destroyed his warships at the Battle of the Nile. He hurried back, and with his soldiers supporting him, set up a new form of government.

From that time, he said, France would be ruled by three consuls. And he would be the First Consul.

NAPOLEON CROSSES THE ALPS

The period in French history from 1799 to 1804 is known as the Consulate. Napoleon was the real ruler of France but it was a very troubled country. There was no money; the South of France was in semi-rebellion, and the leaders argued among themselves. Only Napoleon stood firm.

Austria was besieging Genoa, so the French leader decided to help the latter. He took his army across the Alps and on June 14, 1800, he fought the Austrians at the Battle of Marengo. This proved to be the most brilliant of all his many victories. Six months later the Austrians were defeated again and gladly signed a peace treaty.

The only power that still stood out against him was Britain. He tried to defeat the stubborn little island but due to the British Navy all his efforts failed. Then, with the Treaty of Amiens in 1802, there was peace throughout the world.

INVASION PLANS

A year later, Britain and France were at war again. This time Napoleon threatened to invade. He sent a large army to Boulogne from where the coasts of England were clearly visible, and ordered a fleet of seven thousand flat-bottomed boats to be built to carry his troops across the stretch of water that separated the two countries. But, once again, he was prevented by the British men-of-war on constant patrol.

To take his people's minds off this failure he had himself crowned Emperor of France in the great Cathedral of Notre Dame on December 2, 1804.

The humble Corsican gunner had come a long way!

AUSTRIA ROUTED

In July, 1805, Austria and Russia joined Britain in an

Above left: Trooper, British Life Guards. After a gallant charge at Waterloo, Wellington saluted them as they trotted back with, "Thank you Life Guards."
Above right: Sergeant, Royal Horse Artillery, 1815. This regiment was formed in 1793.

Below: Private, British 13th Light Dragoons, 1814.

Left: French headdresses, 1815. (*top*) Carabinier's helmet. (*left*) helmet of the dragoons of the Guard and (*right*) Polish style helmet known as a *czapka*. In addition to the elegant helmet the carabiniers wore a white coat with light blue facings and a brass cuirass.

alliance against Napoleon. He immediately replied to this by sending his patient invasion army from Boulogne on a rapid march to the Danube. On October 17, he surprised the Austrian Army by his sudden appearance before the walls of Ulm which he took without a fight. He then marched on and on December 2, completely destroyed the Austrian Army at the Battle of Austerlitz.

In 1808, Napoleon designated his brother, Joseph, King of Spain. That country immediately declared war against him. Austria and Portugal joined Spain and Britain. British troops were sent to Spain and the fighting between them and the French became known as the Peninsular War.

THE PENINSULAR WAR

This was the only time in all the wars fought against Napoleon in which British commanders had full control and in which the main body of the army was almost entirely British. There were many Spaniards and Portuguese fighting in this war but they were used mainly as guerillas and commandos.

For a while the British Army was commanded by Sir John Moore who handled a brilliant withdrawal to Corũna. It drew the French armies away from Madrid and allowed the Spanish time to regroup.

Below: Austrian Dragoon. At the time of Waterloo, in 1815, the Austrians were with the Russians on the Rhine.

Left: Trumpeter, French 16th Dragoons.
Far left: Chasseur of the Guard. These chasseurs, with grenadiers, formed the famed Imperial Guard of Napoleon. Both wore similar uniforms – blue coats and tall bearskins – except that the latter wore a brass plate on the front of their bearskins. They were the cream of the French infantry and were only thrown into action when the situation was critical. During the afternoon of Waterloo, Marshall Ney begged Napoleon to send him some of the Imperial Guard to help him. Napoleon refused and an opportunity for a French victory was lost.

Moore died in action and the command was taken over by Arthur Wellesley, who was later made the Duke of Wellington.

WELLINGTON'S TRIUMPHS

For a while Wellington was forced to fight on the defensive. Then in September 1810 the tide turned. He won the Battle of Fuentes de Oñoro and also of Albuera in May. Several smaller battles followed and then in 1812 his army stormed Ciudad Rodrigo and Badajoz, won the Battle of Salamanca and occupied Madrid and Seville.

The Peninsular War ended with the surrender of the French armies in the South of France. By that time the British had won nineteen major battles, taken four great citadels and driven the French right out of Spain and Portugal. In this fighting France suffered 200,000 casualties while the British dead in Spain alone numbered 40,000.

By then, however, Napoleon had foolishly invaded Russia. His army occupied Moscow but he was forced to retreat, losing most of his army.

In April, 1814, Napoleon was compelled to abdicate and was sent to the island of Elba.

Left: Spanish Infantry Private, the Queen's Regiment, 1806. The white of the Spanish uniforms was changed during the Peninsular War to a dark blue coat with gray trousers, while the dragoons wore coats that were mainly yellow.

Far left: Private of the 8th Polish Lancers. The uniform of the Polish Army had been re-styled on French lines, except for the fifteen Lancer regiments which still kept their uniform of dark blue.

Left: French troops 1815. They are (*from left to right*) Foot Artillery and Light Infantry, Privates and a Corporal, infantry of the line. The patterns of these uniforms had changed very little since the 1780's. The main alteration was that the white coats of the old regime had been replaced by the blue ones of the National Guard.

On the morning of Waterloo, Napoleon commanded the finest troops in France. By nightfall his army, broken and demoralized, was streaming away from the battlefield. Even the Old Guard — the elite of his army — had been forced to retreat from the field.

Right: Trooper, French 4th Hussars.
Far right: Trooper, French 11th Cuirassiers. In the hussars, every regiment was clothed differently, although the headdress was the standard shako. The cuirassiers got their name from their steel cuirass, or breastplate. At Waterloo, several squadrons of French cuirassiers were challenged by the British Household Cavalry and the 1st Dragoon Guards. The British cavalry were led by Lord Uxbridge and the shock of meeting hundreds of men and horses was followed by the clang of swords on helmets and corselets. Lord Somerset, who commanded the whole of the British cavalry, remarked that it sounded like "so many tinkers at work!" Most of the time, however, the French cavalry were attacking the British squares. In every case they failed to break them. Of the 15,000 French horse that died that day, nearly every one was killed by shot from the British infantry or artillery.

Left: Drummer, Russian Grenadiers, 1814. In Russia, the basic color for the infantry and artillery was a darkish green. The headdress of most regiments was the bell-topped shako. In 1812 this shako was altered so that the top, which had been flat and level, was curved in the middle and rose at the back and front.

NAPOLEON'S RETURN

With Napoleon safely out of the way on Elba, the leaders of the European nations gathered in Vienna to settle the future of Europe. Before the congress ended, however, the members received startling news. Napoleon had escaped from Elba and had landed in France. As he moved across France toward Belgium, his old soldiers flocked to his standards.

He landed near Cannes on March 1, 1815, with only a few to greet him. By June 15, he had reached Charleroi with an army of 124,000 men and some 350 guns. Even though they had been caught by surprise, the Allies were able to raise an army of 200,000. The Prussian commander Blücher, had 116,000; Wellington, an Anglo-Dutch force of 93,000.

THE BATTLES OF LIGNY AND QUATRE BRAS

Numbers, however, were not everything. Napoleon's army was entirely French, while that of the Allies was made up of more than half-a-dozen nations. "Boney" had supreme command, while the Allies had two commanders – Wellington and Blücher.

Napoleon divided his army in order to thrust a wedge between the two Allied commanders. Blücher's army was defeated at Ligny. Wellington was hard-pressed at Quatre Bras, but managed to withdraw, thanks to the timely appearance of the Light Division. They arrived at Quatre Bras, in time to enable Wellington to pull his forces back to a place he had already selected for the main battle. It was near a small village called Waterloo.

Left: Grenadier of the Russian Army. In the infantry the collar and cuffs were scarlet for all units. The regiments were identified by the color of the shoulder straps.
Far left: Officer of the Don Cossacks. The Russian cavalry was very splendid and included cuirassiers, dragoons, hussars, lancers and, of course, the famous Cossacks, the truly national cavalry of the Russian Empire. The Cossacks played a very important part during the retreat from Moscow in 1812. Warmly dressed, and well mounted, they would appear on the skyline to strike terror into the plodding, ill-clad and half-starved French soldiers.

THE BATTLE OF WATERLOO

The battle began late in the morning on June 18, 1815. The Allied Army was drawn up behind a ridge on one side of the battlefield. Before it were a number of farm buildings, defended by British soldiers. On the other side of a valley were the French. Far away, but marching through mud and rain to reach the battlefield in time was Blücher's Prussian Army.

THE "INVINCIBLES" SUFFER DEFEAT

The battle raged furiously all day. The fighting was particularly fierce around two of the farms. French cavalry charged the British squares, but they held and the cavalry had to fall back, their colorful squadrons thinned by musket and cannon fire.

Right: German troops. (*From left to right*) Gunner, Württemberg Guard Artillery, 1812; Silesian *jäger*, 1815 and Grenadier, 2nd Pomeranian Regiment, 1810.
The Prussian Army had been almost wiped out at the battles of Jena and Auerstadt in 1806, but Great Britain supplied a great deal of clothing to assist in its rebirth. At the time of Waterloo, the various provinces within the Prussian Army were distinguished by the color of collar and cuffs. Thus, East Prussia was red, West Prussia crimson, Pomerania white, and so on. Within each province the regiments were further identified by the color of their shoulder straps, 1st white, 2nd red, 3rd yellow, and 4th light blue.

The long Sunday wore on. At last Napoleon realized that time was running out. The stubborn British would soon be reinforced by the oncoming Prussians. He launched his Imperial Guard – the "Invincibles" – upon the British center. This elite corps toiled up the slope and then, as they almost reached the crest, a long line of scarlet rose up to meet them. It was the British Brigade of Guards.

For a while the soldiers on both sides disappeared in the thick fog of musket smoke. When it cleared the French were in retreat. By nightfall the battle was over. It was a historic victory.

Left: Belgian Carabinier. The Belgians combined with the Dutch at the time of Waterloo. Together they totalled more than 13,000 infantry, 3,000 cavalry and 1,100 artillery.
Far left: Portuguese Caçador, 1812. Caçadors, or light infantry, proved of great value for scouting and guerilla work during the Peninsular War. The infantry of the line wore dark blue jackets and trousers with a tall-fronted shako which may well have been the forerunner of the British Belgic shako

Pages 26 and 27: The glittering French cavalry batter in vain against the British squares at Waterloo.

Above left: Private in the U.S. infantry.
Above right: Sergeant, U.S. Light Artillery. By this time the United States forces were wearing uniforms similar to those of the British, except that nearly all regiments wore blue.

THE FIGHTING REPUBLIC

Although the United States had gained independence, there was still much ill-feeling between the new nation and Britain. This was aggravated when British warships began to search American merchantmen and "press" their best seamen for service in the British Navy. There was also a coastal blockade so that no U.S. goods could be exported.

At last, on June 18, 1812, war was declared. Britain at that time was deep in the Peninsular War. For a time honors seemed even. Then, when Napoleon was captured in 1814, Britain was able to release large numbers of her regular troops for American service.

Several regiments of Wellington's veterans arrived and soon routed the ill-trained and badly led American corps.

AN HONORABLE PEACE

At last, with the northern army in retreat, trade at a standstill and the country bankrupt, the United States was forced to sue for peace. A peace treaty was signed at Ghent, Belgium, but the fact that it had been done so was not known in the South. A battle took place at New Orleans where General Andrew Jackson, with unskilled troops opposed British regulars. He was helped by French pirates who manned his artillery. The British were beaten, losing two thousand men.

Left: Bandsman, British 1st Foot.
This was the oldest regular regiment in the Army. Originally known as Le Régiment de Douglas, it served the kings of France and Sweden before coming into the British Army. By 1812 it had become the Royal Scots. As was usual, bandsmen wore more elaborate uniforms than the rest of the men. They were usually in reversed colors.

THE PEASANTS' WAR

With a large part of Europe involved in the wars of Napoleon, countries in South America decided it was a good time to free themselves from their European masters. The first to do so was the island of Haiti, then belonging to France. The slaves rose up against the rich plantation owners and when Napoleon sent regular troops to crush the rebellion, they were defeated. Haiti became independent.

Another country to free herself was Mexico. This had been conquered by Cortés in 1520 and had been oppressed by cruel governors for centuries. Several risings were defeated until 1822. Although Spanish rule was ended in that year, Mexico was still to suffer years of trouble and unhappiness.

A HISTORIC MARCH

Argentina's story was a happier one. When Napoleon invaded Spain and put her King in prison, the peasants decided to revolt. They took over the powers of the Spanish viceroy, and on May 25, 1810, when the viceroy resigned, a junta, or local government, ruled instead.

Large Spanish armies in Chile and Peru invaded Argentina from time to time, hoping to return it to Spanish rule. Then an Argentine general named José de San Martín, came forward. He led a surprise attack over the Andes into Chile. Argentina won two historic battles to gain independence.

Above left: A peasant in the Mexican militia. The only uniform he wears is his cross-belt and ammunition pouches.
Above right: Private of the Mexican Grenadiers of Toluca. A number of regiments were formed having uniforms copied largely from the French. For a long time Mexico was ruled by revolutionary governments. The soldiers, therefore, wore whatever the general in power at that time decided they should wear or, more frequently, what they happened to have available.

Right: An Argentine *Infernale*. Much of the country of Argentina consists of broad grassy plains called pampas on which vast herds of cattle are grazed. The gauchos — or cowboys — who look after these herds have always been magnificent horsemen. When war with Spain began, regiments were raised which were composed entirely of these hard-riding, hard-fighting cowboys. They formed the backbone of the nation's light cavalry. One corps, founded in 1814, wore coats and tasselled caps of vivid scarlet, a color which earned them the name of *Infernales*, or "Devils". With this colorful uniform they wore the wide, flapping trousers of the gaucho.

THE CADETS OF CHAPULTEPEC

The "Lone Star State" of Texas was first settled by the Spanish. In 1727 the territory was formed into a province and named Tejas, or Texas, after a local Indian tribe. But by the end of the century, Texas was part of Mexico.

In 1835, fighting along the Texas border flared into war when the Mexican general, Santa Anna, besieged the stronghold of the Alamo. When this structure fell, every one of its 183 defenders, including the famous Davy Crockett, was slaughtered.

REMEMBER THE ALAMO!

There was peace for a time, then war began again when Texas decided to become an independent state. General Winfield Scott landed at Vera Cruz and with their cry of "Remember the Alamo!" his troops battered their way forward to Mexico City where, guarding the city, stood the castle of Chapultepec.

Its small garrison included forty cadets of the Military Academy, some of whom were only fifteen years old. The castle was bravely defended and only surrendered when most of the garrison and six of the boys were dead.

War ended with a peace treaty signed in 1848.

Below left: Mexican Infantryman. Such men were recruited from peasants. Their uniforms were modeled after those of the French with similar shakos, black jackets with white cross-belts and blue trousers. Artillerymen wore a similar uniform, but their trousers were red and worn over white gaiters. The gallant cadets of the Military Academy wore blue caps with a red tassel, light blue uniforms with white cross-belts, and a red stripe down the trouser leg. As a nation, the Mexicans were fine horsemen and the pride of their Army was the cavalry. Their uniforms were like their own colorful national costumes; they had large sombreros, jackets decorated with large silver buttons and white braid. Their trousers were of the bell-bottom type in a variety of colors. Over all this they wore gay *serapes*, or gaudy woollen cloaks.

THE CRIMEAN WAR

Below left: Private, British 4th Light Dragoons. This was one of the five regiments which formed the Light Brigade. The others were the 13th Light Dragoons, the 8th and 11th Hussars and the 17th Lancers.

Both the Heavy and Light Brigades were commanded by Lord Lucan. His failure to grasp the state of the battle led to the famous ride into Death Valley.

Below center: Officer, British 19th Foot. This later became the 1st Yorkshire Regiment and, from the green facing on the soldiers' uniforms and from their colonel's name, they also became known as The Green Howards.

Below right: Officer, Royal Artillery. Artillery played an important part in the Crimean War. Some of the guns used in the siege of Sebastopol were very large.

In 1853, Russia had gone to war with Turkey and, afraid that a victorious Russia might upset the rest of Europe, Britain, France and Sardinia went to Turkey's aid. This began the Crimean War. It proved to be the most badly managed war in history. The armies did not have enough supplies, they were inadequately clothed for the bitter Russian winters, and there were no proper arrangements for the care of the sick and wounded.

In 1854, the Allied Armies laid siege to the port of Sebastopol. The Russians attempted to relieve the port but were driven off. During one of these attempts some Turkish guns were captured. The brave, senseless and very well-known Charge of the Light Brigade was the result. An army of seven hundred men attacked the Russian batteries at the end of the North Valley. Only 195 soldiers returned.

THE BATTLE FOR THE ALMA

Before the epic charge at Balaclava took place, a bitter battle had raged for the heights of Alma. It began a week after the Allied Army had landed in the Crimea and was a task for the infantry. The Russians, defending the heights, were in an enviable position of strength, supported by a huge battery which mounted heavy cannon and howitzers.

STORMING THE GREAT BATTERY

The Allied troops, British Guards and line regiments and French Zouaves toiled up the steep cliffs. They were met with a hail of round shot, grape shot and musket fire. The British reached the Great Battery at last. Fighting was fierce here, but the Russians broke when the Highland Brigade came into view. Shortly afterwards the Battery was captured, but 3,300 Allied troops lay dead or wounded on the blood-soaked slopes.

INKERMAN

The final great battle in the Crimean campaign was fought when the Russians tried to relieve Sebastopol. Their attempt began early in the morning of November 4, 1854, in a thick fog which covered the

Above: Private, Russian 31st Infantry Regiment, 1854. His full dress uniform was not worn in the field. Here he covered a gray uniform with a long coat, of heavy gray cloth. Russian cavalry consisted of hussars, cuirassiers, dragoons and lancers. All had elegant dress uniforms.

Left: Trooper, Sardinian Genoa Cavalry, 1855. The uniforms of this army later served as a pattern for the forces of the new kingdom of Italy.
Far left: Turkish officer 1855. Although the Crimean War was fought to save Turkey from Russia, Turkey did very little once Britain and France entered the conflict.

Left: Gunner, Russian Horse Artillery of the Guard, 1855.

whole battle area. The church bells in Sebastopol rang out, their loud clanging drowning the sound of troops and guns moving up into position. At first the Russians broke the outer lines of the Allied position. Then the Welsh and 49th Regiments managed to hold the advance. The huge numbers of the enemy slowly pushed them back but the noise of the fighting warned the rest of the camp.

A GREAT VICTORY

The remnants of the Welsh and 49th had to give way at last but their place was taken by the Coldstreams. The thousands of Russians taking part in this last great struggle began to gain advantage. The British regiments drew back, fighting for every foot of ground. At this critical time the French general, François Cetain Canrobert, with regiments of Zouaves and Line Infantry and a strong force of artillery, began an attack on the enemy flank. The Russians, realizing their defeat, broke and fled.

FLORENCE NIGHTINGALE

This senseless Crimean War cost the lives of several hundred thousand men. Some died on the battle-fields. Most men, however, died from disease or starvation. There would have been more, had it not been for Florence Nightingale. This amazing woman, with her group of women helpers, tended the wounded on the battlefields and devoted her life to hospital reform, not only in the Crimea but later throughout the world.

Above: Private, French 2nd Zouaves, 1854. The colorful Zouaves had begun as a native corps of Kabyles of the Zouaoua Tribe. By the time of the Crimean War, the Zouaves were entirely European but still dressed in the Eastern style. The 1st and 2nd Zouaves served in the Crimea and proved to be first class fighting troops. The regiments were distinguished by the color within the oval ornaments on their jackets.

THE SEPOY RISING

In 1750, the East India Company raised an army to protect its traders and trading posts. A century later this private army had grown into a force of a quarter of a million men. It was divided into three distinct armies – the Bengal, Madras and Bombay. Each of these armies included cavalry, infantry, artillery and engineers. Several regiments of regular British troops were attached to these armies for a tour of duty. The group was known as The Army in India.

A CRUEL RUMOR

For some years there had been unrest in India, with mutinies breaking out in several native regiments. These, however, were overcome by the British troops.

The most serious mutiny of all took place within the Bengal Army in 1857. After a period of grumbling and discontent, an incident occurred which caused the sepoys – as the native soldiers were called – to rise against their British officers.

A new Enfield rifle had just been issued to the troops and to load it, each soldier had to bite off the top of a greased cartridge. The rumor spread that the grease was that of a cow or pig.

Eating these animals was against the sepoys' religion and, horrified, they refused to fire the new rifles. Many were jailed as a result.

MUTINY!

On May 15, 1857, at the large garrison town of Meerut near Delhi, this disobedience turned to open and violent mutiny. British officers and their families were murdered. The sepoys then marched on Delhi. They easily captured the city and then cruelly slaughtered every white person that they found there.

The mutiny spread like a forest fire. Lucknow was besieged. At Cawnpore, the British soldiers with their wives and children were massacred after being told their lives would be spared if they surrendered.

After much fierce fighting, Delhi was retaken and Lucknow reinforced with fresh troops, although it was not until March of the following year that it was finally relieved.

The last battle took place at Kalpi in May 1858. By the end of that year the great Indian Mutiny, which had cost so many innocent lives, was over.

Above: Officer of Hodson's Horse in 1857. He wears the white service uniform generally worn by all ranks during the sultry Indian summer. He also wears the tropical topee. This corps was made up of several independent units in the Punjab which took the name of their founder, Lieut. W. S. Hodson. It was in action at Delhi when the troops wore a khaki uniform with red facings. The word "khaki" comes from the Indian word *khak*, meaning dust.

Pages 36 and 37: The 78th Highland Division in fierce hand-to-hand fighting outside the walls of Lucknow.

Left: Sowar, or non-commissioned officer of the 2nd Punjab Cavalry, later the 22nd Sam Browne's Cavalry. Sam Browne was the Second-in-Command when it was formed. He became famous for his courage, and in some fierce hand-to-hand fighting he lost an arm from a sword cut in the shoulder. Although he was only a lieutenant, his name lives on in the cross-belt for officers which he devised and which is still worn.

Right: Sepoy, 20th Bombay Native Regiment, 1857. The British did not bother to design uniforms in keeping with native dress. The poor sepoy, for the most part, had to swelter in thick uniforms similar to those worn by British line regiments. His hard and heavy shako without a peak was not found in other armies. The sepoys, however, did not take to army boots. They wore sandals or, more frequently, went barefoot!

There were numerous irregular and local corps in the Indian Army at this time. They included the Assam Light Infantry, Oude Infantry, the Gwalior Contingent, Militia, Rangers and the Express Camel Corps.

Far right: Rifleman of the 2nd Gurkhas, 1857. Gurkhas are tough, small men from the Himalayan mountains. They were first recruited by the East India Company in 1815. Later they were formed into rifle regiments, wearing the traditional dark green uniform of that corps. Gurkhas have fought valiantly for Britain ever since. Their national weapon, the *kukri* (a cross between a sword and a knife) is greatly feared by their enemies.

ANOTHER NAPOLEON DECLARES WAR

Sardinia had been an ally of France during the Crimean War. When this was over, and peace had been established, these two countries drew even closer together. At that time Italy was a divided country under the continual threat of Austria and the two Allies decided to do something about this state of affairs.

Napoleon III was the emperor of France and Victor Emmanuel the king of Sardinia. Francis Joseph II was the emperor of the Austro-Hungarian Empire. War broke out in 1859. A large French army invaded Lombardy and the Austrians were badly defeated at Magenta.

ITALY BECOMES A UNITED NATION

Prussia, now a very powerful nation, watched what was happening and began to make threatening moves along the Rhine River. In consequence, an armistice was hurriedly signed between the Allies and Francis Joseph on July 11, 1859.

This was followed by an uprising in Sicily, led by Garibaldi, the Italian patriot. Sicily and Naples were liberated and Italy, except Rome and Venetia, fell to Victor Emmanuel. In 1861 he became the first king of Italy.

The period of this Franco-Austrian war is the most colorful in the history of the French Army. Soldiers

Below left: Hungarian Infantry Private. He wears the mid-blue, close-fitting trousers with short ankle boots. His shako is in a slightly conical shape, smaller at the top than at the base. Cuirassiers and dragoons of the Hungarian cavalry wore white tunics while light blue overalls were being worn in 1840. Hussars wore uniforms of light or dark blue. This varied according to the regiment. The shakos also varied, being white, green or scarlet.
Below right: Austrian *Kaiserjäger* Officer. The light infantry – or *jäger* – was formed as early as the Seven Years' War. At this time they were clothed in gray-green uniforms called "pike-gray."

of the Imperial Guard, for example, were dressed in more elegant uniforms than ever. It seemed as if the nephew of the great Napoleon Bonaparte was determined to outdo his uncle. The French Imperial Guard was more resplendent than ever. There were lancers in dazzling white, blending with light blue and scarlet; guides and chasseurs in green and gold; dragoons and cuirassiers in shining brass and steel.

THE BATTLE OF SOLFERINO

The army commanded in person by Francis Joseph had suffered defeat at Magenta. It retreated across the Mincio River and regrouped around the old city of Verona. Early on June 24, when neither army expected to meet the other, they suddenly clashed at the Mincio. The Franco-Sardinian Army numbered 150,000 men; the Austro-Hungarian, 160,000.

The battle began very early in the morning. At 7 A.M., Napoleon, who was watching the action from a church tower, ordered his main forces to advance on the town of Solferino, situated on a strongly defended hill. The French Guards went in and after desperate hand to hand fighting, the town was captured. The loss of life on both sides, however, was appalling.

THE FRENCH GAIN THE VICTORY

Now that they were firmly positioned on this rise, the French had the advantage. It became the Austrians' turn to try to regain the town and they made some desperate attempts to do so. All were driven off with further loss of life. At 2 P.M. Francis Joseph gave the order to the general commanding his 1st Army to drive toward the south. Again, every attempt failed.

At this time the French artillery was using a new and deadly weapon – cannon with rifled barrels.

THE RED CROSS IS BORN

Later in the afternoon a severe thunderstorm began. At its height, the Austrians retired. The French were too exhausted to follow, and so the battle ended. By chance, a Swiss citizen, Jean Dunant, was near the battlefield. He was horrified to see so many wounded men dying for lack of attention. When he returned to Geneva he called a meeting of other influential men. From this meeting the International Red Cross was formed.

Above: Cantinère. For many years women had gone to war with the regiments to act as nurses, cooks and laundresses. They usually wore their own clothes or discarded uniforms. In the French Army, in 1859, they eventually acquired status and had their own delightful uniforms.

THE WAR OF THE DANISH DUCHIES

It often happens that provinces on the borders of two powerful countries become victims of a political tug-of-war between those countries.

This was the lot of the three frontier provinces of Schleswig, Holstein and Lauenberg. They lay between Prussia and Denmark and had been a source of contention for a long time.

PRUSSIA DECLARES WAR

In 1848, the Germans living in these duchies rose against Denmark, hoping to gain independence. They had the moral support of both Prussia and Austria. After a while, Bismarck, Prussia's chancellor, was not content to stand by, and he declared war on Denmark.

The great non-German powers of Britain, Russia and Sweden began to interfere, threatening to support Denmark. Bismarck had to give way and the duchies remained firmly with Denmark.

Right: Warrant Officer, 4th Magdeburg Field Artillery Regiment. Although the pickelhaube was now the standard headdress of the Prussian Army, the artillery wore a ball instead of a spike. The light infantry — the *jäger* — wore a dark green uniform with red collar-patches. They also wore a helmet at first, but this was replaced by a tall conical shako with a peak at the back and front.

Right: Officer, Prussian Dragoons of the Guard. The cuirassiers were in white, and the hussars, as usual, in uniforms of different colors for every regiment. The lancers, or uhlans, wore the usual uniform of Polish origin.
Far right: Officer, Austrian 27th Infantry Regiment. The Austrian infantry had now replaced the cylindrical shako with a conical type, which was not unlike the French kepi. In the field, however, it was worn with an oilskin cover.

THREE AGAINST ONE

On November 15, 1863, Frederick VII, the popular king of Denmark, suddenly died. He was succeeded by Christian IX and, once again, the German-speaking peoples of the duchies began to press for independence. Britain and Sweden hinted that they would go to the help of Denmark if attacked; Prussia was not yet strong enough to take on all three powers.

THE INVASION OF DENMARK

Bismarck was not content to let matters rest there. In particular, he wanted the fine harbor of Kiel, in Holstein. He sought the help of Austria and thanks to his brilliant statesmanship, drew her to his country's side. On February 1, 1864 the Prussian and Austrian Armies crossed the Eider River into Schleswig.

Bismarck had not meant to invade Denmark, but on February 18, some Prussian hussars on patrol crossed the border and occupied a Danish village. None of the non-German powers made a move, and that was enough for Bismarck.

He sent Prussian and Austrian troops moving over the border and defeated the Danes at Düppel.

The war was soon over. Denmark, alone matched against Prussia and Austria, surrendered on July 12. She later signed away all her rights in the three duchies.

Right: Danish troops. Guide and Infantry Private. The latter were dressed in dark blue kepis and tunics, piped red, with light blue trousers. The Austrian dragoons and hussars wore light blue tunics with a "Roman" helmet for the dragoons and a shako for the hussars. Saxon and Hanoverian troops entered Holstein on December 24, 1863. The Danish troops withdrew to Schleswig. Prussia then invaded Schleswig without warning and the fighting began. The Danish Army had been modernized but they were greatly outnumbered and their equipment was inferior. Nevertheless they put up a very stubborn and gallant fight. They retreated to the Dannevirke fortifications, but superior numbers and training forced them to yield.

THE BLUE
AND THE GRAY

By the year 1850, the United States had become divided into two distinct regions. The North was prosperous and modern. The South had changed very little over the years. In some parts of the deep South, indeed, time seemed to have stood still. Its wealth still came mainly from the vast cotton fields. Thousands of negro slaves toiled in them daily. People in the North, however, hated slavery. This hatred grew, for thousands of migrants, seeking a better life, were pouring into the North from Europe where slavery had been abolished for a long time.

FEDERALS AND CONFEDERATES

In 1860, Abraham Lincoln was elected president. The following year, however, the seven cotton-producing states, South Carolina, Georgia, Florida, Alabama, Mississippi, Louisiana and Texas formed themselves into the Confederate States of America and elected Jefferson Davis as their own president. Tension grew.

The first clash came on April 12, 1861, when Fort Sumter, garrisoned by only seventy Federals – as the Union troops were called – was besieged by a

Below left: Private of the 5th New York Zouaves. There were an amazing number of these zouave regiments on both sides. The uniform was based on those first met by Allied forces during the Crimean War. This style of uniform crossed the Atlantic and caught the imagination of Federals and Confederates alike. Some units copied the French almost exactly, such as the Ellsworth Zouaves and the 5th New York. Both wore blue jackets and scarlet breeches. Hawkin's New York Zouaves were in dark blue throughout. The Wallace Zouaves of Illinois favored light blue; Berdan's Sharpshooters were dressed entirely in grass green and the Massachusetts Iron Brigade was dressed in light blue with black felt hats. A further regiment to adopt another country's uniform was the 79th Cameron Highlanders. This was a body of Scottish volunteers who borrowed not only the British regiment's title but its number as well. It took its name from its colonel, James Cameron. In May 1861 nearly 900 strong, it marched with pipes playing down Broadway on its way to war. Two months later it was routed at the First Battle of Bull Run.
Below right: Cavalry Officer. Horses played an important part in the Civil War. The men of the South, in particular, were usually magnificent horsemen.

Confederate force. The garrison was forced to withdraw. Blood had been shed, which meant war must follow.

The Civil War was to rage for four long and desperate years, during which more than two thousand battles were to be fought.

FIRST BATTLE OF BULL RUN

The first important battle was fought near a small stream called the Bull Run. Here 70,000 men had their first taste of war, for hardly any of the soldiers had been in action before. The Union troops dressed mainly in blue uniforms, the Confederates in gray.

Above: A typical Federal bandsman. Every infantry regiment had its drummers. Often they were young boys who were not old enough to shoulder a musket. His task was to beat calls or orders, for the noise of battle often drowned an officer's shouted commands. Drummers wore colorful uniforms with plenty of gold braid, so that the officer could easily pick them out from the rest of the men.

Left: Gunner, 1st Tennessee Artillery.
Far left: Drum Major of the 1st Virginia Regiment, a Confederate Regiment. Although most regiments were composed of hastily assembled volunteers, the uniforms of their bandsmen were often as magnificent as the one he wears. Bandsmen, in all countries, always wore more colorful uniforms than the rank-and-file. This was true even in the more soberly clad Northern regular regiments.

43

The First Battle of Bull Run proved to be one of the strangest in history. It ended with a rout of the Union forces, but their opponents were so disorganized that they were unable to pursue them.

This victory gave the Southerners a feeling that they were far better fighters than the men of the North. This was to prove fatal. The Northerners, learning from their defeat, began to take the war very seriously. New officers were appointed and fresh armies trained.

BROTHER AGAINST BROTHER

As the war went on, other states entered the war. Virginia, North Carolina, Tennessee and Arkansas joined the Confederacy. Missouri, Kentucky and Maryland sided with the North. This meant that in some of the battles of this terrible war, fathers fought against their own sons, or brother against brother.

THE WAR GOES ON

At first, the odds seemed about even. There were twice as many people in the North than the South; there were factories to produce guns and munitions; the Northerners had a larger navy. But the forces of the South were fighting on their home ground, were better trained and, at first, had better leaders.

The goal of the northern armies was to try to capture the Confederate capital of Richmond, Virginia, gain control of the Mississippi River and blockade the southern ports. Such attempts were defeated by General Robert E. Lee, aided by "Stonewall" Jackson. Northern forces were beaten at the Second Battle of Bull Run. Lee then invaded the North, but was driven back.

THE LAST SHOT

The Confederates slowly lost ground. General Ulysses S. Grant led an army west and gained control of most of the Mississippi River. Vicksburg, the last Southern stronghold, was starved into surrender. Then General Robert E. Lee attacked the North once more. He was defeated at Gettysburg. In 1864, General Grant became commander-in-chief of the entire Northern Army and his men gained victory after victory. Both of these great generals met to discuss surrender terms at Appomattox Court House, Virginia. The war was over at last.

Above: A member of the Virginia Cavalry. At the beginning of the Civil War conditions were similar to those in Britain during the Civil War of two centuries earlier. Wealthy planters, like the noble cavaliers, furnished their own horses and led their own men into battle.

Right: The Battle of Gettysburg marked the turning point of the Civil War. General Robert E. Lee, leading the Confederate Army, invaded the North as far as Gettysburg. But the Union Army, under General George G. Meade, held a strong position, and after three days' fighting, defeated the Southern forces.

Right: Private of the Louisiana Tigers, a Southern Zouave regiment. The Zouaves were especially popular in the Southern states as there were many French-speaking people in these former French colonies. In fact the dress of the Louisiana Zouaves was an exact replica of the orignal French uniform. On the other hand, so were some of the uniforms of the zouave regiments of the North. This must have led to considerable confusion on the field of battle!

Far right: Sergeant of the Mississippi Rifles. On both sides, the old muzzle-loading musket had been replaced by the breech-loading rifle. The infantryman could now shoot further and more accurately than before, and could load without having to stand up!

THE IRON CHANCELLOR

In 1859, Wilhelm I, King of Prussia, appointed a new minister of war. Count Otto von Bismarck, who in time became one of the most powerful men in Europe. He was clever, cunning and loyal. He later became known as the "Iron Chancellor" because nothing and no one could bend or break him.

After Waterloo, where the Prussians had been Wellington's Allies, the scores of small kingdoms and duchies of Germany began to group together into one large federation. Prussia, of course, was at the head.

BISMARCK'S PLANS

Bismarck was not satisfied with things as he found them. He wanted these loose-knit quarrelling states to be more than a federation. He wanted them to be one great nation with his king ruling as emperor.

First he had to test the strength of the Prussian Army. A victory would make the other countries take notice of the new nation he was helping to create. In 1866, Prussia declared war against Austria.

In a campaign that lasted for only seven weeks,

FRENCH MILITARY UNIFORMS IN THE 1870's
Below left: Officer of the Garde Mobile. As the Franco-Prussian War continued, the great losses in the French Army were filled by reserves of the Garde Mobile. This was mainly an infantry body and was to prove a most valuable asset. The men were clothed in the style of the times but in light blue trousers with a broad scarlet band.
Below center: Rating of the French Navy. At the outbreak of the war, France had one of the most efficient navies in the world with forty-nine iron-clads compared to Prussia's five.
Below right: Algerian "Tirailleur." To keep the Army up to strength, Napoleon called in colonial troops including the Zouaves, "Turcos," and the Tirailleurs Algeriens. The Tirailleurs distinguished themselves in a memorable action at Wissembourg in Alsace. A strong Prussian regiment had to attack the southern gate of the city. The Algerians checked the advance three times, but were finally crushed by heavy cannon and rifle fire. A memorial marks the spot where they fell.

Austria was completely smashed at the Battle of Sadowa and the Austrian Emperor was forced to give up the position his ancestors had held for centuries in Germany.

A new era was to begin. And Bismarck was ready.

A SHADOW OVER FRANCE

Napoleon III was becoming uneasy at the growing power of his neighbor. Sadowa had proved that the Prussian Army was a force to be respected. But France was not in a strong position. She had supported Archduke Ferdinand Maximilian in Mexico. Money and troops had been poured into that country. The scheme had failed and her soldiers were now returning to France.

FATEFUL AUGUST

It slowly became obvious that war would soon erupt between France and Prussia. Napoleon thought that he would be supported by Italy and Austria.

Neither of these hoped-for Allies was willing to join France against Prussia, so Napoleon decided to act alone. He found an excuse to declare war on July 19, 1870, but it was some time before his unprepared army was ready to move.

Left: Officer of the Saxon Infantry. He wears the typical spiked helmet — pickelhaube — worn by all except the Bavarians. Each state had a different helmet-plate to distinguish it from others. Prussia had an eagle; Saxony a star; Baden a griffin, and so on. Most uniforms were based on the Prussian design: dark blue tunics and almost black trousers.
Far left: Private of the Bavarian Infantry. He wears a type of helmet unique to his country. It has a black fur crest in place of the spike.

Below: Trumpeter, Prussian 11th Uhlans. Uhlans were one of the crack German regiments. Their main weapon was an ash lance, their uniform Polish in design.

During the fateful August of 1870 he personally led his army out to meet the German divisions that had crossed the frontier into Alsace and Lorraine. The first clash came when one of Germany's three armies defeated their enemies at Wissembourg and, two days later, at Wörth. Another Prussian army routed a strong French corps. War had begun with a vengeance and already France seemed to be in strife! These first victories were followed by three fiercely fought battles before the fortress of Metz, which was held by the French, under Marshal Bazaine.

GRAVELOTTE SAINT-PRIVAT

This was the most decisive battle of the three. It was also the first time that the bulk of both armies met in combat. Helmuth von Moltke commanded an army of 179,000 infantry, 24,500 cavalry, and 730 guns. Bazaine had approximately 140,000 men with 450 guns and mitrailleuses.

One part of the battle was fought in and around a large cemetery and an assault on this position cost the Prussian Guard 8,000 casualties in twenty minutes!

By nightfall the Germans were advancing; by midnight the battle was over. The French were forced out of Saint-Privat, but the victors were too tired to pursue. Bazaine, with the remnants of his army fell back on Metz.

The Germans besieged Metz on August 19, and on August 29, it surrendered.

THE BATTLE OF SEDAN

The victory of Saint-Privat meant that Bazaine, safely behind the walls of Metz, was unable to join another French army under Marshal MacMahon. Realizing this, MacMahon broke camp at Châlons and marched to relieve the besieged city.

He fought the battle of Beaumont on August 29 and the Battle of Musson on the following day. He lost both and fell back on Sedan. On September 1, he was completely surrounded. During the early evening the French were forced to take a stand within the city while countless hordes of Germans swarmed up to surround it on all sides. They were commanded by the King of Prussia.

This was too much for Napoleon who was also inside the walls of Sedan. A white flag was hoisted and he surrendered as a prisoner of war to King Wilhelm.

Above: Private of the Baden Infantry. The contingent from Baden, together with those of Bavaria, Saxony, Würtemberg and, of course, Prussia, formed the main part of the German Army. Colors of uniforms worn were similar. The exceptions were riflemen of the *jägers* who wore a shako with a green tunic.

The Prussian Guards were the finest drilled regiments in the world. This was demonstrated at Saint-Privat where, without flinching, they stolidly marched into withering rifle fire.

THE END OF THE WAR

The Battle of Sedan cost Napoleon his throne and France a large part of her army. The fall of Metz was another terrible blow. Yet France fought on, for she still had some armies left. Paris was besieged. The city began to be shelled and every attempt to relieve it failed. With its surrender the war ended, and Wilhelm of Prussia was crowned Emperor of Germany.

Bismarck's plan had succeeded.

Right: Prussian Cuirassier Trooper. His white uniform was even worn in action. The helmet reverts to the English Civil War period with its long "lobster" neck-protector. These troopers were part of the Heavy Brigade. The two regiments of Bavarian Heavy Riders and the Saxon Carabiniers were in the same class. At the battle of Mars-La-Tour, Cuirassiers of the 7th Regiment of Seydlitz and the 16th Uhlans lost more than half their men when they charged the French guns. The remainder overran the guns and raced on until faced by two fresh brigades of French cavalry. This charge was to become known as "Von Bredow's Death Ride."

WAR IN CUBA

By the end of the nineteenth century, Cuba was one of the few remaining possessions in the New World still under Spanish rule. For a long time there had been arguments between the once great empire and the new, proud republic. On February 15, 1898, the battleship, *Maine* was lying in Havana Harbor. Suddenly there was a huge explosion. When the smoke cleared away the shattered hull of the warship was sliding slowly beneath the surface, taking 266 lives with her. No one ever found out who was responsible, although it was believed to have been caused by a Spanish mine.

SPAIN DECLARES WAR ON AMERICA

On February 20, the United States demanded that Spain withdraw her troops from Cuba. She also began a blockade of the island's harbors. Four days later Spain declared war.

Although it was mainly a sea war, the U.S. Army was expanded. A call went out for volunteers. The rallying cry was, "Remember the *Maine*!" Soon a large army was ready to leave Tampa Bay for Santiago, Cuba. It proved to be a nightmare embarkation, for the port was too small to handle the flow of thousands of men struggling to board the troopships. But they landed in Cuba at last, and troubles became worse. The roads were bad, there

Above left: Rough Rider in field uniform. This regiment fought bravely under their colonel, Theodore Roosevelt, who later became President of the United States. They attacked a strong force of Spaniards near San Juan Hill. Roosevelt led a cavalry division on foot in an assault on the enemy outpost. From this new position he led his brigade across a valley, up a steep hill and into the enemy's stronghold. This charge of the Rough Riders, who were joined by the 1st and 10th Cavalry — also dismounted — became a famous action.

Above right: U.S. Light Artillery Officer in full dress uniform.

Right: Spanish Infantry Private and (*far right*) Cavalry Officer of the Princesa Hussars. The hussars were dressed in light blue with a white pelisse and kepi. The Pavia hussars wore a similar uniform except that the tunic was red and the pelisse light blue. The kepi was also a darker shade of blue.

The cavalry was made up of hussars, lancers and light cavalry. The lancers wore a light blue hussar tunic with black braiding, with a red collar and pointed cuffs, also of red. They wore a steel helmet with a spike and other fittings in brass. The light cavalry had a similar uniform except that they wore a light blue kepi with a red band at the top.

Below right: Gunner, Spanish Artillery. The Spanish tropical kit consisted of a white linen uniform with blue stripes. With this they wore a straw hat that was not unlike that worn by British sailors at this time. Infantry uniform for field service at home, however, was very similar to that of the French. It had red trousers and a blue-gray turned-back greatcoat. Instead of epaulettes the Spaniards had red shoulder pads in the form of "wings." They also wore their distinctive traditional footwear which laced up the leg.

At the time of the embarkation for Cuba, the United States Army was being issued a khaki uniform for field service. This was to be worn with the flat-brimmed felt hat. Few of the troops sent to Cuba, however, had these before they sailed. Most of them were in the blue field uniform which had been adopted in 1880. The cavalry and infantry full dress of the United States Army at this period was very similar to that of the British, especially in the spiked helmet. The helmet-plate of this was in the form of a brass American eagle. It had been hoped to equip the troops with a new rifle called the Krag–Jorgensen. Unfortunately, enough of these were not available at first and the volunteers went into action armed with the old single-shot Springfield rifle firing black powder. The same telltale powder was fired by the few U.S. field guns that were used in Cuba. They were inferior to the Spanish guns which fired a smokeless powder that did not give away their position. Also, few of the military departments operated very well. But this was the first time that the United States had sent an army overseas. Much was learned from this experience.

were few supply wagons, and as the men moved inland, resistance grew stronger.

After a hundred-days campaign, however, Spain stopped fighting and gave up all claims to Cuba.

THE WAR MOVES ON TO THE PHILIPPINES . . .

The war was not merely confined to Cuba. The Philippine Islands were also under Spanish rule. Six warships of the Asiatic Squadron eventually appeared outside Manila, under the command of Commodore George Dewey. The city was then besieged for some time by Major General Wesley Merritt with a force of about 20,000 men. The Spanish were forced to surrender on May 13, 1898.

. . . AND PUERTO RICO

The United States forces then turned their attention to Puerto Rico. The invading force consisted almost entirely of volunteers of the National Guard, the only exception being the 10th Pennsylvania Infantry. There was little fighting, for the Spanish surrendered with hardly a shot being fired. In general the Puerto Ricans welcomed their new masters with enthusiasm.

When peace was signed on August 12, 1898 over 300 years of Spanish rule in America came to an end.

WAR AGAINST THE BOERS

As early as 1652, Dutchmen had been settling in southern Africa in the region of Cape Town. Settlers from other nations joined them and adopted their language. By the end of the Napoleonic Wars in 1815, the colony at the Cape came under British rule. British settlers arrived and the Boers – who were colonials of Dutch descent – decided to make a new home. Some 12,000 trekked across the Orange River and in time founded the two republics of the Transvaal and the Orange Free State.

UNION CAUSES DISUNION

For a time Britain recognized the independence of these two republics. Then, in 1867, diamonds were found. Although the Boers had claim to the rich diamond fields, Britain took them over. In 1877, she also took possession of the Transvaal in an effort to bring about the union of the whole of South Africa. Gold discoveries in the Rand brought thousands of gold-greedy settlers to the area, and more troubles.

THE JAMESON RAID

In 1890, Cecil Rhodes, who gave his name to Rhodesia, used his position as Prime Minister to organize an armed raid into the Transvaal. He sent his friend, Dr. Leander Starr Jameson, to lead a raiding party into Boer territory, but the raid failed and Rhodes resigned.

Above: British Infantry, 1900. Private of the Highland Light Infantry (*top*) and Sergeant in the Rifle Brigade.

Left: Sergeant, 6th Inniskilling Dragoons, 1900.

These are shown in full dress uniform For the Boer War, however, and for the first time, the troops fought entirely in khaki. They also wore the Wolseley type of pith helmet.

BRITISH DRESS UNIFORMS AT THE TIME OF THE BOER WAR

For special occasions in Britain, and
sometimes in South Africa during a lull
in the fighting, the British soldier at
this time could don very colorful
uniforms. The cavalry, except for the
Royal Horse Guards, together with
hussars and lancers, wore scarlet tunics.
In addition, the Life Guards, Dragoon
Guards, and Dragoons wore helmets,
the Royal Scots Grays the bearskin. The
infantry of the line was also in scarlet.
At the time of the Boer War it was
wearing a dark blue helmet with a brass
spike and a star-shaped plate, bearing
the regimental badge in its center.
Fusiliers wore the raccoon-skin cap and
the light infantry a dark green helmet.
Rifle regiments were in their traditional
very dark green, with a small black fur
cap. Highland regiments wore kilts in
their appropriate tartans with the
exception of the Highland Light
Infantry which wore light infantry
uniform with trews of the Mackenzie
tartan.

This raid caused the antagonism between the two
nations to deepen. At last, in 1899, the long expected
war broke out, which was to last for two years.

SOLDIERS VERSUS FARMERS

The British in South Africa thought that the Boers,
most of whom were farmers, would soon ask for
peace. They were shortly made aware that their
opponents were brave men and expert marksmen.
The Boers won many victories and besieged several
towns. The most important of these were Kimberley,
Ladysmith and Mafeking.

Seasoned troops had to be sent from Britain to
carry on the struggle. They were commanded by
Lord Frederick Sleigh Roberts with Lord Horatio
Kitchener as his Chief of Staff.

The war dragged on until a peace treaty was finally
signed in Pretoria on May 31, 1902.

THE BOXER REBELLION

The Dowager Empress of China hated foreigners. If she could have had her way they would all be killed or thrown out of her country. She felt, with some justification, that the great powers were seizing territory that rightly belonged to her people. The Emperor, Kuang Hsü was a weak man. In 1898, she deposed him and became the ruler of the vast, sprawling Chinese empire.

THE BOXERS

The Empress learned of a strange secret society whose Chinese name meant "fists of righteous society" but which the Europeans called the "Boxers." She spoke to their leaders and told them that it was her wish that they attacked the "foreign devils" whenever they could. She would give them her support if it was needed.

THE ATTACKS BEGIN

By this act she hoped to rid the country of all foreigners, yet, if questions were asked, she could say that the murders had been done by unknown bandits.

Crowds soon flocked to the banners of the Boxers who began to attack defenseless and isolated Christians. Churches were burned down and every white person they found in these out-of-the-way communities was killed without mercy. The Boxers'

Below left: Sepoy, 3rd Sikhs and (*right*) Sapper, Bombay Sappers and Miners. The British contingent included a number of Indian troops sent over from the nearest possible bases. Their uniform, as at the time of the mutiny, was very similar to that of the British Army. Their head dresses, however, were very native in style while the Sikhs looked very impressive with their full beards. Indian troops were the first to enter Peking. They were men of the 1st Regiment of Sikhs and the 7th Rajputs.

Indian Sappers and Miners, like those in the British Army, wore the red tunic of the Royal Engineers with blue facings. They were, in fact, the colors of the Royal Artillery in reverse. The red, dark blue and yellow were repeated in the turban. The breeches, of dark blue with a scarlet band, were the same as those worn by the gunners.

courage grew with their numbers and they began to march northward to where most of the foreigners lived. This was in the capital, Peking. Within this ancient city the foreign ministers and their staffs lived in legations – one to each country – eight in all.

THE TAKU FORTS

At this time a number of foreign warships were lying off the Taku Bar at the mouth of the Pei Ho River. The British admiral, Sir Edward Seymour, had received an urgent cable from his legation and decided it was time for action. He worked out a plan with the other foreign admirals – there were eight different nationalities altogether. Guarding the entrance to the river were four large forts. They were being heavily reinforced with troops and Seymour knew that if they could close the river, the naval squadron would be useless.

ATTACK – BRITISH STYLE

The nine ships of the small squadron moved nearer the forts, whose Chinese commander was told that he had twenty-four hours in which to surrender to the Allies. Twenty-three hours later the forts suddenly opened fire. Seven of the ships returned this fire but two destroyers, *Whiting* and *Fame*, moved past the forts and then cast off whalers, filled with armed bluejackets. Sometime later, landing parties went ashore from the other ships, by which time, however, the forts were badly damaged. By dawn all four forts had surrendered.

Above: Gunner, Royal Marine Artillery. Royal Marines played an important part in the defence of Peking. At one time a number of Chinese had set up a post near some burning houses and were firing into the British defences. Captain Halliday led a sortie of Marines against them and fierce fighting took place among the burning buildings. He was severely wounded, but was able to return to the legation. For his bravery in this action he was awarded the Victoria Cross.

Left: Non-commissioned officer, German Marine Artillery. "Horse Marine" jokes have been prevalent, but this regiment of mounted artillerymen was actually part of the marine corps. Men of the German Army were heavily engaged during the Boxer Rebellion and a German warship, the *Iltis*, was in action against the Taku Forts. Over five hundred Germans formed part of the 2,129 men of Admiral Seymour's column which captured a huge Chinese arsenal near Tientsin. Later, when the arsenal was evacuated and the men moved on to reinforce Tientsin, twelve of their number had been killed and sixty-two wounded.

An officer and fifty-one men of the German Army helped defend Peking. A German naval detachment of some one hundred officers and men took part in the relief of the city.

WAR DECLARED

The Empress was told of the fighting at Taku but she was not told of the outcome. Thinking that it had been a Chinese victory, she sent out a general call to arms. China had declared war on the world!

The Grand Army of the North was ordered to march upon Peking and attack the legations. When they were captured, her gallant army, and the Boxers, had her permission to slaughter every "foreign devil."

FIGHTING AT TIENTSIN

There was now no law or order anywhere in China. At Tientsin, where there were a number of foreign settlements, the Boxers were causing trouble. Regular Chinese troops with artillery also arrived, and the tiny garrison had to defend a five-mile perimeter against a force of ten thousand regulars and Boxers.

The defenders fought from behind barricades made of bales of merchandise. They were shown how to build these protective walls by a young American mining engineer, Herbert Hoover, who would in later years become President of the United States.

A week after the fighting began a relief force arrived. It included British regular soldiers and a number of Americans, Russians and Germans. This force reached Tientsin just in time to save the hard-pressed defenders from being wiped out.

Above: Infantry and Marine Officers of the United States Army. Although at this time the United States was engaged in the war in the Philippines, her troops in China rendered valuable service. There were 2,000 in the International Relief Force, or one-tenth of the whole. They had their own mules and large Studebaker wagons and were much envied by men of other armies who had hardly any transport at all. The United States Marine Corps at this time wore a uniform very similar to that of today. The tunic then was double-breasted, but the light blue trousers, with the scarlet band, are identical.

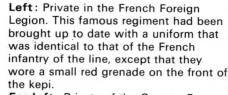

Left: Private in the French Foreign Legion. This famous regiment had been brought up to date with a uniform that was identical to that of the French infantry of the line, except that they wore a small red grenade on the front of the kepi.

Far left: Private of the German East-Asia Brigade. This brigade was made up of three infantry regiments, one squadron of light cavalry, one field artillery detachment, one company each of pioneers and transport, medical services and three battalions of marines. In the infantry, the regimental number was shown on the shoulder straps. Colonial troops of the German Empire had uniforms of khaki and wore either the standard pith helmet or a felt hat turned up at one side. The International Relief Force that marched to Peking was commanded by a German — Field-Marshal Count Alfred von Waldersee.

Below: Chinese Boxer. The members of this society were not regular soldiers and therefore had no recognized uniform. A description of one of them is given as: "A full-fledged Boxer with his hair tied up in red cloth, red ribbons round his wrists and ankles, and a flaming red girdle tightening his loose white tunic."

PEKING PREPARES

In Peking, at this time, the members of the various legations were busily preparing for a siege. Even before the fighting became general, there were many incidents. The German Minister was murdered in the street and no one in authority bothered to punish his assassin. Other groups of Boxers attacked the Austrian Legation but were driven off by machine gun fire.

Outside the settlement, however, thousands of Christians were murdered. Realizing that they were cut off from the rest of the country, the Europeans in Peking were busy digging trenches, putting up barricades and collecting food.

THE DEFENDERS

Within the legation area in Peking the members of the different nations realized that the time would soon come when they would have to fight for their very lives. It would be a most unusual instance of international cooperation.

There were some regular troops among the people of the legation area and they were to bear the brunt of the fighting. They numbered twenty officers, 389 men, and seventy-five volunteers. Half of the latter were Japanese ex-servicemen.

This tiny force had the task of defending more than three thousand people, including women and children.

DEEDS OF BRAVERY

The center of the defense was the British Legation. When fighting began on June 21, 1900, Sir Claude MacDonald, the British Minister, was chosen to command the defending forces.

He led men of eight nations. There were British, Americans, Germans, Russians, French, Austrians, Italians and Japanese. These men fought together, performing many gallant deeds during the fifty-five days that the siege lasted. In the desperate fighting that took place on the walls of the legation area, the defending forces would often be made up of soldiers from three and sometimes more different nations.

As they fought, the International Relief Force was battling its way up from Tientsin. On July 14, it entered Peking. The siege was over.

THE BEAR AND THE DRAGON

The Great Bear of Russia was stirring restlessly. It was looking hungrily toward the east and new territories. At the same time, however, the Dragon of Japan, newly awakened from centuries of mediaeval existence, was looking toward the west. Not believing that Japan would dare to challenge her might, Russia began to pour troops into Siberia, a relatively simple matter, since the Trans-Siberian railway had just been completed. While the troops were still on their way, a powerful Russian fleet steamed into Port Arthur to take possession of this important ice-free harbor.

A NEW JAPAN

These moves naturally upset Japan, but no Russian notice was taken of her protests. Russia had not yet realized that Japan had changed from a backward nation of simple peasants and fierce war-lords into one ready to take her place in the modern world. Her Navy was British-trained. Her Army was drilled by German officers.

She could get no satisfactory reply from Russia. Russia seemed intent on ignoring her. In 1902, therefore, Japan signed an alliance with Britain which was to last for five years.

Russia was next asked to withdraw her troops from Manchuria before October 1903. In October, however, Russian troops remained and Russian ships still swung at their moorings in Port Arthur.

The Dragon was ready to breathe fire. During the night of February 5, 1904, Admiral Heihachiro Togo launched a surprise attack on the Russian fleet.

THE BATTLE OF PORT ARTHUR

When Admiral Heihachiro Togo had confined the Russian fleet, he gained command of the sea. This meant that Japanese troops could be landed without interference. Some of the troops were put ashore to engage a strong Russian Army. The remainder were used to besiege Port Arthur.

This harbor was exceptionally strong. It was sur-

Below: Russian troops.
Left: Gunner of the Horse Artillery.
Center and right: Private, 1st Regiment Lithuania and Officer in the undress uniform of the 12th Dragoons. By 1882 the Russian Army had become entirely reorganized and re-equipped. All the cavalry except the guard was changed to dragoons, and the colorful lancers and hussars disappeared until 1912 when, once again, they were to be seen in their full splendor. The Cossacks, however, remained unchanged. The infantry wore mainly dark green uniforms with tall boots and small fur caps for dress occasions. In the field a flat round cap without a peak was worn.

At Port Arthur the Russian infantry, huddled behind battered walls of the forts, often saw the Japanese advancing across open ground. Machine-guns and magazine rifles mowed them down in hundreds. It was the first time that such concentrated fire had been utilized in battle.

rounded by a chain of hills and defended on all sides by walls and forts.

By the end of July, however, the Japanese Third Army had occupied all the outlying positions around Port Arthur. On August 7, the first shells began to fall into the city itself. The Dragon's claws had closed on their prey.

DESPERATE FIGHTING

The Russian fleet also came under attack. It tried to escape, but Togo was waiting. After a brief action, one battleship struck a mine and was sunk. The rest ran back to the harbor or to the safety of a neutral port.

For a time there was a lull, then fighting began again in September with an attack on a stronghold called 203 Metre Hill. Here the soldiers clashed with rifle and bayonet in hand-to-hand combat. The Russians defended the position stubbornly and were not overthrown until the end of September.

The attacking forces crept forward a few vital yards every day. Fighting was savage and the loss of life appalling. One by one the Russian positions were overrun by Japanese infantry shouting their battle cries of "Banzai!"

On January 3, 1905, after a six months' siege, Port Arthur surrendered. For the first time in modern history an Eastern power had defeated a Western nation.

Above: Japanese troops. Gunner, Coast Artillery and (*right*) Private, Infantry of the Guard.

During the siege of Port Arthur the Japanese artillery brought up immense guns which pounded the town with 11-inch shells. Destructive 110-ton mortars were also used. Casualties during the six-month siege were high — the Japanese had nearly 100,000 casualties.

THE BALKAN WARS

There had been a time when the great Ottoman Empire had ruled almost all of the near-Eastern world. Then, as the years passed, its borders slowly shrank, although at the beginning of this century, its empire still included many provinces which had no common ties with their Turkish rulers.

The surrounding nations, closer to these provinces than Turkey herself, waited for the chance to wrest them from her.

The opportunity came in 1912, when Turkey, weak from a recent war with Italy, was ripe for attack. Tension grew during the year as Greece, Serbia, Bulgaria and Montenegro formed the Balkan League. In October, hostilities began.

FIGHTING ON THREE FRONTS

From the outset the Turks were in a difficult position, since they were forced to fight on three fronts at the same time: on the Bulgarian frontier in Thrace, on the Greek frontier in Macedonia and on the Serbo-Bulgarian border.

The brunt of the conflict fell upon Bulgaria, who had the strongest army. She had nine divisions which

Above: Turkish Light Infantry Sergeant. His badges and collar-patches, etc., are green. The line regiments were scarlet.

Left: Troopers of the Bulgarian 3rd Cavalry Regiment.

meant that she could send some 180,000 men into the field. In a campaign that lasted three weeks, the Bulgarians gained the victory of Kirk Kilissa on October 24, 1912, defeated the Turks again at the Battle of Lule Burgas, and finally forced the main Turkish Army to fall back on the defenses of Constantinople, the Chatalja lines.

On March 26, 1913 Adrianople fell into Bulgarian hands and with its surrender the war was virtually over.

THE SECOND BALKAN WAR

A treaty was signed in London on May 30, 1913. This gave the whole of Turkey in Europe, except Constantinople, to the Balkan Allies. But the ink was hardly dry when the old jealousies and hatreds between the Balkan countries broke out again. The victors were soon squabbling over the division of the spoils of war.

This led to the Second Balkan War. This time Greece and Serbia were joined by Rumania and fought Bulgaria. This campaign lasted for only one month then Bulgaria, utterly defeated, was forced to sign away everything she had won in the previous war, and much of her own territory as well.

At the same time, the Turks had retaken Constantinople and got back a great part of Eastern Thrace. Greece was given Crete and most of the Aegean Islands. This comparatively short war had altered the map of Europe.

Above: Serbian troops. (*Left to right*) Cavalry Trooper, Artillery Gunner and Infantry Private. The cap and footwear are peculiar to the Serbian Army.

Above: Evzone, or Light Infantryman. He wears the picturesque national costume which exists to this day; it is worn by the National Guard in Athens.

THE GREAT WAR 1914-18

Less than a year after the Balkan Wars ended, more trouble in that part of Europe was to lead to the most far-reaching war so far experienced.

There were some provinces in the Austro-Hungarian Empire which had a number of Serbian-speaking peoples. Some of these formed secret societies plotting for Serbian independence. On June 28, 1914, the Archduke Franz-Ferdinand, heir to the Imperial Throne, was shot by an assassin while riding through the streets of Sarajevo.

Austria immediately demanded satisfaction from Serbia, who in turn sought aid from Russia. This was what Germany had been waiting for. As an Ally of Austria she was bound to oppose any move by Russia, who, in turn, was allied to France. There was a flurry of activity in high circles until, on August 3, 1914, France and Germany declared war.

BRITAIN ALSO DECLARES WAR

In order to outflank her age-old enemy, Germany thrust her troops through neutral Belgium. Great Britain, who had sworn to defend Belgian neutrality, sent an ultimatum to Germany. On August 4, Britain was also at war with the German Empire.

This came as a surprise to Germany who had thought that Britain would stay out of the conflict. She was not much concerned, however, for she knew that Britain's "contemptible little army" could easily be destroyed.

In that fateful summer of 1914, seven European nations were marching to war. Four years later almost the whole world was in arms.

THE WESTERN FRONT 1914

When war began in the West, opposing forces were evenly matched. The first series of battles became known as the Battle of the Frontiers. In these battles approximately 3,500,000 men took part.

The German plan was to hold the French with half of their strength and drive the remainder through Belgium into northern France. The Germans

Above: Private, French Infantry of the line, 1917. When the French infantry mobilized for war, the soldiers went in campaign dress and even wore the red trousers and kepi. Indeed, service dress in the French Army had hardly altered since 1870, but it soon became obvious that a new type of uniform was required. The general cut remained the same but the color was changed to horizon blue. This was supposedly to merge with the landscape.

Right: Staff Sergeant, Royal Scots Grays, the only mounted regiment in the British Army to wear the bearskin cap. His uniform was only for ceremonial occasions, of course. In the field, British cavalry also wore khaki. Many regiments still carried the lance.

Center: Territorial, 11th London Regiment (Finsbury Rifles), a typical British "Tommy" in khaki service uniform. In 1914 he was part of a small army, but one which was the best trained and equipped in Europe. His main weapon was the Lee Enfield SML Mk3 rifle. In addition to this he carried ammunition pouches, a canteen, bayonet and entrenching tool. His dress uniform was green with scarlet facings.

Far right: Officer of the East Riding of Yorkshire Yeomanry, 1914, another famous Territorial unit.

Below: Trooper, the Australian Light Horse, 1914. Every man was a volunteer and provided his own mount. There were twenty-three regiments, all dressed in the same style of uniform. They were to distinguish themselves in many notable actions, especially at Gallipoli in the Dardanelles. Like so many other countries in the British Empire, Australia was quick to answer the call to arms.

marched into the densely forested country of the Ardennes and on August 22, clashed with the French. The battle lasted for two days. The French, driven back with heavy losses, began to retreat to the River Marne.

Erich von Falkenhayn, chief of the German General Staff planned one big offensive for 1914 which would capture Calais. The German Fourth Army, however, was stopped by the small British Army amid the blood and mud of Ypres. The German attack failed and troops on both sides began to dig in.

THE EASTERN FRONT 1914

While the Allied armies were fighting it out with the Germans on a line which ran from Belgium to Alsace–Lorraine, other battles were being fought on the Eastern Front between Germany and Russia.

The Russian strength lay in her vast numbers. With millions of men under arms, she hoped to steam-roller her way over all opposition.

THE BATTLE OF TANNENBERG

The campaign opened with the First and Second Russian Armies crossing the East Prussian border. Two battles were fought, at Gumbinnen and Stalluponen, both claimed as Russian victories. The German commander was then replaced by a famous general – Paul von Hindenburg.

His arrival put new life into the German troops who now swung over to the offensive. Leaving one Corps to hold the line, Hindenburg sent the rest of his army to trap the Russian Second Army amid the forests and lakes around Tannenburg. The Russians were defeated, thousands of prisoners being taken, and the Germans then swung to the east, smashed the First Army and hurled it out of East Prussia.

BARBED WIRE AND TRENCHES

The winter of 1914 saw the opposing armies on the Western Front facing each other in trenches that snaked from Switzerland to the sea. They sheltered five million men. Occasionally units would climb out of the trenches to cross No Man's Land in an attempt to gain a few yards of ground. They rarely succeeded. Bullets and shells scythed them down. Barbed wire strung before the trenches proved another cruel hazard.

French and Germans died by the thousands in the Champagne area, the British at Neuve-Chapelle. The Second Battle of Ypres brought the horror of poison gas. The closing months of 1914 brought the Battles of Loos and Vimy Ridge, to end three months of slaughter.

Above: French troops, 1914. An Alpine Chasseur and a Private, Infantry of the line, before the change to light blue uniforms. The chasseurs fought in the Vosges and acquired the name "blue devils." All French infantrymen were armed with the Lebel rifle.

Left: Officer, King's African Rifles, 1918.

Far left: Officer, the New Brunswick Scottish of Canada. Apart from its own regular troops, almost every dominion had a number of Scottish units, most of them being allied to a parent regiment in Scotland.

Right: Officer, 19th Chasseurs à Cheval, 1914. Like the dragoon officer, his regimental number is shown on his collar. The French, in common with most other European nations, expected too much of their cavalry arm. The lessons of the Boer War had not been learned – that a horse makes a big target for a rifleman or machine-gunner and that once a horse is down the cavalryman is at best a second-rate infantryman. It was only realized later, also, that the cavalryman, while always over-eager to fight, could no longer charge *en masse* as in the days of Napoleon. Machine-guns and artillery made such attacks suicidal.

Far right: French Artillery Gunner. He had 75-mm field guns, the most advanced piece of artillery of its time. The breech mechanism was a masterpiece of technical design.

THE TRAGEDY OF THE DARDANELLES

It was resolved, in view of the stalemate on the Western Front, to begin operations elsewhere. With her command of the sea, Britain planned an operation which would finish Turkey, help Serbia and Russia, and perhaps persuade Greece and Bulgaria to join the Allies.

Above: Trooper, French Dragoons, 1914. The French cavalry consisted mainly of cuirassiers, dragoons, hussars and chasseurs. At the outbreak of the war, all cavalry arms wore a kind of full dress. The cuirassiers even continued to wear their helmets and steel breast-plates, although they covered them with a khaki cloth to prevent reflections by the sun from exposing their positions!

On February 19, 1915, a force of battleships entered the Dardanelles and shelled the Turkish forts. The army then went ashore. It was made up mainly of men of the ANZAC – the Australian–New Zealand Corps. The landings were made at Cape Helles. Many soldiers were shot down as they stumbled ashore, others before they could dig shallow trenches. Stalemate again. By January 1916, the survivors were evacuated, the scheme a disaster.

WILDERNESS OF MUD

1916 was the year of two of the greatest battles of all time. They were the attack on the French forts at Verdun and the Battle of the Somme. In February, German guns began to bombard a ring of forts around Verdun which, a year before, had been stripped of most of their heavy armament.

The German guns thundered away and then,

Above: Belgian uniforms, 1914. (*Left*) a Chasseur (Light Infantry). The infantry had Mauser rifles and Berthier light machine guns drawn by dogs. (*Right*) Artillery Officer. The Belgian Army, led by their King Albert I, put up a brave resistance against the German onslaught It was greatly outnumbered and in spite of British support had to fall back to the River Yser.

Left: Russian troops, 1914. (*Far left*) Sergeant, 1st Siberian *Jägers*. A new uniform had been designed for the Russian Army in 1913. Plain service dress could be changed into full dress by merely buttoning on a colored cloth front and the appropriate collar and cuffs. These were yellow for grenadier units and crimson for the *jägers* (or light infantry). The cap was made of gray lambskin with a khaki top. Some regiments bore the small brass scroll, worn as a battle-honor. (*Left*) Officer, Horse Artillery of the Garde du Corps. The distinctive shako worn by this officer is a modification of the bell-topped model of the early nineteenth century.

thinking that no one could have lived through such a deadly storm of steel, the German infantry went in to the attack. To their surprise, dazed men rose out of the ruins to fight back. Other attacks also failed. At last by December, the Germans reluctantly withdrew. Verdun had held.

The Battle of the Somme began on July 1. Shells from either side churned up the ground until it became a mass of huge, water-filled craters. The British fought side by side with their brothers-in-arms from Canada, Australia, India, New Zealand and South Africa.

In September a British attack was launched with a new and secret weapon – the tank. Its appearance startled the enemy who found that their bullets made no impression on these rumbling, iron-clad monsters. But there were too few of them to achieve much and the element of surprise had been thrown away.

By the end of 1916 the Allies had lost about 1,200,000 men, the Germans 800,000. It was not so much a war – as sheer slaughter.

"THE YANKS ARE COMING!"

By 1917, those countries which had been at war since the beginning in 1914 were feeling the strain. Their regular troops had nearly all been killed, yet still the cry was for more and more men to fill the gaps.

Above left: Serbian Cavalry Officer. In 1914, Serbia had mobilized half a million men together with another 50,000 from Montenegro. They were attacked on August 12, by three Austrian armies. The Serbs, with the experience gained in the Balkan wars, met them with courage. In less than two weeks the Austrians were forced out of Serbia with the loss of 50,000 men. The Austrians returned in December and captured Belgrade, the Serbian capital but it was retaken two weeks later.
Above right: Portuguese Infantry Private. Portugal entered the war in 1916. She fought on the side of the Allies but mostly in Africa.

Left: Trooper of the Belgian 4th Lancers.

The Germans decided to pull back from their trenches to more strongly fortified positions known as the Hindenburg Line. This could be held with far fewer men than the trenches, thus saving manpower, while presenting the Allies with a harder nut to crack.

An attack on the Hindenburg Line was opened at Arras. It began with a moderate victory when the Canadians captured Vimy Ridge. At the same time the French were launching a tremendous attack on the Aisne. This was a disaster from the very first day. By the end of May it had fizzled out with no gains for the French but with the loss of 120,000 of her men.

The French troops needed rest, and so the British were told to hold the enemy until their Allies could return to the trenches. The result was the Third Battle of Ypres fought in a nightmare of mud, stench and rotting bodies.

Then, to the exhausted Allies came fresh hope. The United States of America had declared war on Germany. The first of her troops arrived during June 1917. By the end of the year the "Yanks" were pouring into Europe to assist the war-weary Allies, while across the Atlantic, factories were producing guns, tanks and aircraft – the sinews of war.

THE LAST GREAT OFFENSIVE

At the beginning of 1918 Allies and Germans alike

Above: United States troops, a Sergeant and a Private.

Above: American Artillery Trumpeter 1914. The United States entered the war on April 2, 1917. For service in France her troops wore khaki service dress which was almost identical to that of the British, except for the felt hat.

Right: German troops, 1914. The German Army at the outbreak of war was the best equipped and, with the exception of Russia, the largest in the world. In 1914 she had seventy-eight divisions. (*Right*) Officer, 35th Brandenburg Infantry Regiment. He wears the new field-gray service dress in which the German infantry marched to war. Colored piping and similar ornaments were used to identify a particular regiment. The full dress of the Brandenburg Regiment, however, like others in the Army was far more colorful. It was the regulation dark blue tunic and black trousers with a red collar, shoulder straps and cuff slashes and with the regimental number in yellow on the shoulder straps. Well-trained and equipped, the infantryman was the backbone of the German Army. At first he wore the pickelhaube type of spiked helmet. This was later replaced by a soft, peak-less cap and then the steel helmet. Mauser Gew 98 and 98K were the standard infantry rifles used by the German Army throughout the entire war. (*Far right*) Drummer of the Bavarian Leib Regiment. The infantry side-drum he carries is of a very shallow pattern and was introduced in 1854. There was no Royal Guard in Bavaria, but the Leib-Infanterie Regiment served that purpose. The Bavarian uniform was basically light blue throughout the twenty-three regiments.

were worn out by the war and exhausted. The Germans, particularly were coming to the end of their manpower, recruiting boys and old men. But Erich von Ludendorff, their Commander in Chief, decided to gamble everything on one great offensive. The first of a series of giant hammer-blows fell on March 21. Thousands of shells ripped and tore at the British positions. Then, under cover of a fog, the

Left: Japanese Infantry Private, 1914. His army had been modernized since the Russo-Japanese war. Japan declared war on Germany in 1914, but her war effort was comparatively limited.
Far left: Italian Bersagliere, 1916. He wears the famous ornamental rooster-tail feathers of this regiment in his helmet. Italy declared war on Austro-Hungary, but not Germany, on May 24, 1915.

Left: Trooper, Prussian 9th Uhlans, 1914. The German cavalry was composed of uhlans, cuirassiers, dragoons, hussars and mounted rifles. In the German Army the uhlans were the elite of the elite. They were similar to the British lancers but, like them, were also useless in the face of concentrated fire.

gray clad German infantry moved forward. The Second Battle of the Somme had begun.

At first the Germans were successful for the British front-line trenches were over-run. But the British fought back stubbornly and by April 5, the sound of battle died away.

Four days later the Germans attacked again at the Battle of Lys. This time the British troops were ordered to fight to the end. The savage attacks beat upon their tattered lines but with little success. Towards the end of April, the fighting died down again.

There was a lull on the Western Front until May 27. The third great German onslaught hit French troops and pushed them back across the Aisne.

THE END . . . AND THE BEGINNING

By June 6, the German advance had been halted once more. This was helped by a counterattack launched by U.S. troops at Belleau Wood. On July 15, the Second Battle of the Marne began. This was to be the last German effort, for since March they had lost a million men with little to show for it.

On August 8, the Canadian and Australian troops went into battle behind five hundred tanks and with air cover from eight hundred 'planes. The German front could not withstand such an onslaught. It broke, and the spirit of the men broke with it.

On November 11, 1918, the Germans were forced to sign an armistice. The Great War was over. The Allies had won. They now had the difficult task of winning the peace.

Right: Private, Prussian 10th *Jäger* Battalion. This battalion had seen service in Gibraltar and the soldier wears that battle-honor on his cuff.
Far right: Gunner in the 32nd Saxon Field Artillery Regiment. Most of the German artillery wore the regulation dark blue tunic. The Saxons, on the other hand, wore green. Gunners of both countries had the ball, rather than the spike, on top of their helmets.

Left: Austro-Hungarian Cavalry Trooper of the 11th Hussars, 1914. He wears the full dress of his regiment. In the field, however, the Army generally wore the pike-gray color that had been worn since the Franco-Austrian War of 1859. Hungary was the home of the hussar and this arm, with its sixteen regiments, formed the main part of the Imperial and Royal cavalry in 1914. There were also several Hungarian second-line regiments dressed in blue tunics and pelisses with red lacing and white fur.

MILITARIA

MILITARY HEADDRESSES

Up to the end of the eighteenth century, military headwear was usually a version of the tricorne, although various types of helmets were worn by the cavalry. As uniforms became more elaborate so new designs and styles were introduced. Sometimes the headwear was of a national character which was copied by other nations. Thus the French kepi was soon seen in Denmark, Russia, the United States, and many South American republics.

The spiked helmet, originally worn by warriors of Eastern nations, was not only worn in Germany but also in Great Britain, Russia, Spain and many other countries. The hussar busby was based on the national fur cap of Hungary. In 1805 it was adopted in Prussia and later became the standard headdress for all units.

After the Treaty of Paris, some headdresses became enormous, topped by huge feathers or plumes.

1 Austro-Hungarian grenadier cap of the early 19th century
2 French busby of the First Empire
3 Austro-Hungarian helmet
4 British "belgic" cap
5 Russian dragoon helmet, 1900–14
6 German helmet, 1917
7 Norwegian guardsman's hat, 1900–14
8 Bavarian officer's helmet, 1914

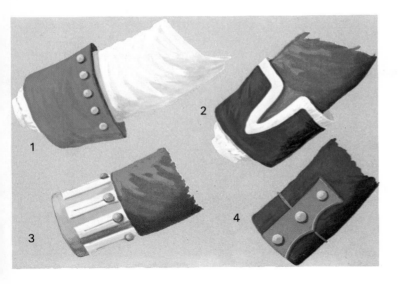

SELECTION OF CUFFS
1 French cuff, early 18th century.
2 British cuff, mid-18th century.
3 British cuff, 1812.
4 French cuff, time of the First Empire.

EPAULETTES
No one knows the origin of epaulettes. They started as very small ornaments in the eighteenth century and grew larger until by the twentieth century they had become very large indeed. The plain shoulder straps were merely to stop the belts and slings from slipping off the shoulders.

Below: (*top row, left to right*) 18th century, general pattern; French First Empire; French, 20th century. (*2nd row*) Various shoulder straps. (*3rd row, left*) British cavalry, mid-18th century, (*right*) British volunteer's wing, late 18th century. (*Bottom row*) German shoulder-strap and drummer's "swallow's-nest", 20th century.

CUFFS, EPAULETTES AND SHOULDER STRAPS

The uniforms of Marlborough's time were merely a form of civilian clothes with a few alterations. Then, because of experience gained in action, they became modified.

The original cuffs were designed so that they could be lowered in cold weather to protect the hands. This was important in the case of infantrymen who could not go through the difficult performance of loading a rifle with frozen fingers!

The buttons were to keep the cuffs in position. To save wear and tear on the buttonholes they were strengthened with loops of braid. Later, when buttons became merely ornamental, these loops were kept as a form of decoration. There were other ornaments which were generously used in dress uniforms. Cavalry uniforms, especially, were often heavily decorated with gold and silver buttons, lace and fur.

Although these colorful uniforms were not very practical, they were frequently worn in action where their brilliant colors could be seen through the thick smoke of battle.

These fine additions and small "differences" gave each soldier a sense of what can aptly be called – *esprit de corps* – or pride in his officers, his regiment and himself.

INDEX

Figures in bold type refer to illustrations and captions

355.1
ALL
    Allen, Kenneth
    Fighting men and
    their uniforms

DATE DUE

355.1
ALL
    Allen, Kenneth
    Fighting men and
    their uniforms

DATE DUE	BORROWER'S NAME
NO1 '78	
NO9 '78	
JA18'79	

DEMCO